My Cooking Story

I started out very young. I've always loved different foods and wanted to learn how to cook. I started by asking questions to the people who did most of the cooking, mama, my foster moms, my grandmother, her friends, and my aunt. By me having a good taste for what I liked it wasn't hard for me to take or add to any recipe I was given to fit my taste. A little of this, and a little of that. When I'm in my kitchen cooking, I'm in my own world. I call it my "Kitchen Therapy"
I wear an apron, and I get busy!

At first, I wasn't knowledgeable about what healthy foods were. It was always about how good the food tasted to me and not how good it was for me. As time went on and I got older I had to change the way I ate, which meant no fried food, no fast food, no processed meats, little to no red meat, leaner cut meats with no fat or skin, and less butter. A saying I have... "If the meat doesn't look like it was cut right off the cow or pig, then the meat was processed."

It was highly suggested I eat chicken breast, turkey breast, and healthy fish options. Also, to eat whole grains, more veggies, fruit, and eat less to no sugar; as in candy, cookies, donuts, cakes, and pies. Drink plenty of water, no sodas, potato chips, and limit my salt intake to 1,500 milligrams per day.
Exercise, exercise and some more exercise!
I do the best I can with it, and some days are better than others. The recipes in this book I cook in moderation, holidays and special occasions for family and friends and also, 'me" time. I really enjoy cooking meals for myself too!

If you are a good cook too, you can add and take away any part of my favorite "Main Dish" recipes you like. Less salt, take out the smoked meat, use ground beef instead of ground turkey or use no meat at all. **Fresh herbs are one of my go-to options as well. You can also use no-salt seasoning options. There are some pretty tasty no-salt seasonings in the stores!!!**

From My Kitchen To Yours!

First and foremost, I want to thank the God of my understanding.

Special Acknowledgement to my three children for encouraging me to make this book of my favorite recipes, and to my son for the big push to finalize and publish it.
I love y'all so much!

I also want to thank my family and friends for your patience and support in my efforts to finally get this done. Thank you!!

Table of Contents

Desserts

Main Dishes and Side Dishes

Miscellaneous

Measurements

Serving sizes for the main dish recipes in this book are for 2 servings unless specified.

A dash/pinch	1/8 tsp. or less
3 tsp.	1 tbsp.
2 tbsp.	1/8 cup
4 tbsp.	1/4 cup
4 oz.	1/2 cup
8 oz.	1 cup
16 oz.	1 lb.
1 cup of liquid	1/2 pint
2 cups	1 pint
2 pints	1 quart
4 cups of liquid	1 quart
4 quarts	1 gallon

Tsp. = is one teaspoon

Tbsp. = is one tablespoon

lb. = pound

NOTE: To avoid scratches in your Teflon/Non-stick pots or pans always use Silicone non-stick heat resistant utensils, not metal or stainless steel.

*If a recipe requires you to bake, for the most part the rack will go in the middle of the oven.

Desserts

This Is It 7-Up Cake

What you will need:
3 cups sugar
3 sticks of real butter (Unsalted)
3 cups (Cake flour)
2 tsp. pure lemon extract
6 eggs
¾ cup of 7-Up (let can or bottle sit out overnight/unopened)
Non-stick spray cooking oil
Bundt cake pan
Powdered sugar – for drizzle
Mixing bowls/one small and one large
Hand mixer/very thin soft spatula or butter knife

Let eggs, 7-up, and butter sit out overnight. Must be room temperature. The next day with the hand mixer cream butter and sugar together in the large mixing bowl. Add one cup of cake flour and 2 eggs, mix well, then add one more cup of cake flour and two more eggs, and mix well, then add the last cup of cake flour and 2 eggs and mix well. Add 7-Up and lemon extract and mix until blended well. Pre-heat oven to 350°. Spray bundt cake pan with oil, and lightly flour using the cake flour. Pour cake mix in the bundt cake pan and cook for an hour or until done. Stick a toothpick in the middle of the cake, it should come out clean when done. Let the cake sit for 30 minutes, then flip bundt cake pan upside down on the cake platter and lift (You may need to take a thin soft spatula or a butter knife to loosen the edges before flipping)
Drizzle: Take some powdered sugar and 7-Up and place them in a small bowl. Mix to the consistency of icing. (Keep adding powdered sugar if needed). Use a small baggie and clip a very small hole in the corner and squeeze over the cake.

Not The Butter Banana Applesauce Bread

What you will need:
4 very ripe bananas (Mashed)
1 cup sugar
½ cup unsweetened applesauce
1 tsp. pure vanilla extract
2 large eggs (Beaten)
1 ½ tsp. baking powder
¼ tsp. baking soda
½ tsp. of cinnamon
¼ tsp. salt
2 cups all-purpose flour
Non-stick spray cooking oil
1 9x5 loaf pan
Electric mixer
Potato masher
Mixing bowl
One large spoon
¼ cup chopped walnuts (Optional)

Pre-heat oven to 350°. Put all the dry ingredients **except sugar** in a bowl and set aside. Place mashed bananas and sugar in a large bowl and stir with a spoon. Let this sit in the bowl for about 10 minutes, then add applesauce, eggs, and stir again. Add remaining dry ingredients and continue to mix with the electric mixer (Just until blended together). Spray the pan with non-stick cooking spray and pour the mixture in it. Bake for 1 hour or until done. (When you put a toothpick in the middle, and it comes out clean). Let bread sit for 10-15 minutes before removing from the pan. *Yum!!!*

English Toffee

What you will need:
1 cup of sugar
1 cup of butter
¼ cup of water
½ tsp. salt
1 bag of semi-sweet chocolate chips
Cooking thermometer
1 15x10 jelly roll pan (See picture)
1 small plastic or heat resistant spatula
1 medium pot

Cook on medium heat, the butter, sugar, water, and salt. Cook until 295 degrees stirring constantly (Or until it reaches the color in the picture). The longer you cook it the browner it will get. When you have reached the brownness, pour into the pan and let it cool for a few minutes, then sprinkle semi-sweet chocolate chips on top and spread. Cool completely. (About an hour or more) before breaking into pieces.

Whipped Peach Pie

What you will need:
8 Fresh (Colorado peaches) peeled and sliced (In Minnesota they usually come out in about mid-August)
20 large marshmallows
8 oz. container of whipped topping
1 deep dish pie shell (brown crust first)
½ cup milk
2.5 qt. double boiler (Use this so you don't burn the marshmallows)
Strainer
Plate (To set the strainer on)

Place pie shell in the oven for 15-20 minutes to brown. Take it out and set aside. Peel and slice peaches, place in a strainer and set aside on a plate. Place marshmallows and milk in the top part of the double boiler, and about 2-3 cups of water in the bottom part. Stir until melted and smooth, (cool a little) then add whipped topping to the mix. Gently stir in the peaches and spoon into the browned pie shell. Refrigerate for 3 to 4 hours before eating.

If You Want To (Cheat) Peach Cobbler So Good!!

What you will need:
1 8x8 baking dish (non-stick works best)
2 deep dish pie crusts
1 29 oz. can and one 15 oz. can of sliced peaches in heavy syrup
½ tsp. nutmeg
1 tsp. vanilla extract
Non-stick spray cooking oil
Unsalted butter (to dot on top)
1 cup sugar
1 medium size pot

Spray bottom of non-stick baking dish with cooking oil and take one crust out of the tin place it on the bottom of the baking dish (Just tear some of the sides if needed) and bake 15-20 minutes or until lightly brown. Pull it out the oven and sit it to the side.

Pour the large can of peaches in the pot including the juice. Only use ½ the peaches in the small can and no juice. Add the vanilla, sugar and nutmeg to the pot and put heat on medium high until it comes to a boil. Carefully pour mix in the baked crust. Tear the other pie crust up and place it on top of the peaches. Cut about six small dots of butter and place all around in different places of the crust. Sprinkle the whole cobbler with a little sugar and then nutmeg. Bake at 350° for 45-1hr. or until crust is brown. *(Picture below was not cooked in a non-stick baking pan.)*

Crushed Pineapple Upside Down Cake

What you will need:
1 box of yellow cake mix
¾ stick of unsalted butter
1½ cups of brown sugar (Light brown)
1 9 x13 baking pan
1 large cookie sheet to flip it on
1 20 oz. can of crushed pineapple (Drain the pineapple and use the juice for the cake mix.)
1 cup of pineapple juice (From the can of crushed pineapple)
Mixing bowl
Hand mixer
1 strainer, and a bowl for the pineapple juice
Parchment paper

Strain the pineapple and set the juice from it aside (should equal 1 cup)

Mix the cake mix as instructed on the box **using the pineapple juice you drained from the crushed pineapples instead of using water.**

Melt the butter in a pan and shift from side to side to make sure it's evenly on the bottom of the pan. Sprinkle brown sugar evenly and add the crushed pineapple evenly. Pour the cake batter over the pineapple mix. Bake as directed on the cake box.

Wait 30 minutes before flipping on to the cookie sheet lined with parchment paper and cool (This way is used if you are going to eat it right away)

NOTE: You can also flip into another baking pan if it's larger than the one you baked it in (This way it can be covered to eat later)

Pumpkin Pie Cake Surprise

What you will need:
1 box yellow cake mix
1 **clear** 9x13 baking pan with a lid
1 15 oz can of pumpkin
½ cup evaporated milk
½ cup heavy cream
3 eggs
1 cup light brown sugar
1 tsp. pumpkin spice seasoning
Non-stick spray cooking oil
Hand mixer
1 large mixing bowl/medium bowl with a lid for the frosting

Use the instructions on the cake box for the cake. Pour the batter into a lightly oil sprayed 9x13 baking pan and set aside.
Mix the remaining ingredients until smooth and pour over the cake batter evenly as you can. Pre-heat oven to 350 and bake for 50-60 minutes. What a surprise! **The pie filling sinks down to the bottom, and the cake is now on top.** Cool completely before putting the frosting on.

Frosting – *Make first and place in the fridge (You can even do it the night before)*
You will need:
1 3.4 oz box of instant vanilla pudding
1 tsp. pumpkin spice
1 cup cold milk
8 oz. whipped topping
Mix the dry pudding, pumpkin spice, and cold milk in a bowl until smooth, then stir in the whip cream. Cool for a about an hour before putting the frosting on the cake.

Must Be This Sweet Potato Pie

What you will need:
2 regular size ready-made pie crust (Pre-bake at 350 for 15 minutes before adding mixture)
7 medium size sweet potatoes or yams
3 tbsp. unsalted butter
½ cup white sugar
½ cup dark brown sugar
2 eggs beaten
¼ tsp. nutmeg
¼ tsp. of cinnamon
¼ cup of evaporated milk
1 tbsp. pure vanilla extract
1 large pot
1 large mixing bowl
Hand mixer

Peel and cut potatoes into large squares and boil, turn heat down to low and cook for 20-25 minutes until tender. Beat eggs and set them to the side. Place sweet potatoes or yams in a large bowl, putting the butter in first so it can melt. Cool a little then mix the remaining ingredients with the hand mixer. Pour into pre-baked crust and bake at 350° for about 45 min.-1 hour or until set. If pies start to get too brown around the edges, put some aluminum foil around them.

From The Island Key Lime Cake

What you will need:
Yellow (Butter) cake mix
¾ cup orange juice (with some pulp)
9x13 baking pan
Mixing bowl
Hand mixer
Prepare as directed on the box, but instead of using water, use the ¾ cup orange juice
Key lime juice (Comes in a bottle)

Icing

In a separate small bowl mix together until smooth:
¾ cup powdered sugar
¼ cup key lime juice (I usually get this when I go to Florida, but I'm sure they sell it in stores.)
Mix to the consistency of picture below
When the cake cools, take a toothpick and stick about 10 holes in different places on the cake, then drizzle the icing over it.

NOTE: If the icing is not the consistency like shown, add more powdered sugar.

Pour the icing in a sandwich bag and cut a very small hole off the corner to drizzle the cake.

Main Dishes & Side Dishes

Black-Eyed Peas and Okra Over Rice

What you will need:

½ small bag of black-eyed peas
4-quart pot
1 tong
1 small smoked turkey leg or smoked meat of your choice
¼ cup chopped onion
½ bag of frozen cut okra
Seasoning salt (Last) the meat may have enough salt in it
Dash of cayenne pepper (optional)
1 cup cooked rice (cook separately)
½ Pot of water

Instructions: Wash peas and take out any bad ones; set aside. In a 4-quart pot half filled with water, wash and place your smoked turkey in and let it come to a boil. Turn the heat down to medium low and cook the turkey leg for about 2 hours with the lid on it. Check occasionally to make sure you there is still water in the pot. If not, add a cup or two of hot water. When the turkey starts to fall off the bone, using the tong take the meat out of the pot and place it on a plate until it cools, then remove the bones. Place the meat back in the pot, add the peas, and chopped onion. Cook on low with the top on for about an 1 ½ hours. The last 15 minutes add cut okra and sprinkle all across the top of all the peas to let it cook. (Do not stir the okra in with the peas) When done, spoon it over the rice.

Jazzy's Breakfast Pie

What you will need:
9" Deep dish pie pan
1 small skillet (for sausage)
1 pan (for hashbrowns)
1 large bowl
7 eggs
Salt and pepper to taste
Garlic powder to taste
1 cup sliced fresh mushrooms
1 cup of frozen cubed hash browns (cooked as directed on the package and set aside)
¼ lb. ground breakfast sausage (Optional)
¼ cup of shredded cheddar cheese to sprinkle on top or inside (Optional)
Small amount of chopped onion
1 cup fresh chopped spinach
Non-stick spray cooking oil
1 tbsp. grapeseed oil

Crumble and place the sausage in the skillet. Cook hash browns, according to the package. Set them aside. In a small skillet sauté spinach, onions, and mushrooms in the grapeseed oil for about 5 minutes on medium high. Drain off oil, if necessary, cool, and mix all the ingredients together in a large bowl. Spray the pie pan with a little non-stick spray cooking oil and pour the mix in. Bake at 350 for about 30-35 minutes or until done in the middle. You will be able to see the firmness of the pie in the middle when it's done. Slice like a pie and enjoy! You can have this with a bowl of fruit on the side if you wanted to.
NOTE: You can also cut Yukon potatoes in thumbnail size squares and fry in grapeseed oil; set on paper towels. Cool before putting them in the mix, instead of the frozen potatoes.

Picture below shows a larger pie pan, and cooked with no cheese or sausage

Oxtail Stew

What you will need:
1 2lb pack of oxtails
I 14.5 oz. can stewed tomatoes (Undrained)
1 10.5 oz. can tomato soup
Black pepper (To taste)
3 carrots sliced into large pieces
2 celery sticks chopped into large pieces
4 russet potatoes (Cut into large squares)
½ rutabaga chopped into medium size squares (if you're not using potatoes, see picture)
½ onion (chopped in large chunks)
¼ bag of frozen cut green beans
3 beef bouillon cubes
2 finely chopped garlic cloves
A dash of seasoning salt **(last)** only if it is not seasoned enough.

Place oxtails in a 4-quart pot and cover the meat with water with the top off. When it comes to a boil pour all the water off (this takes out some of the grease) Add fresh water to cover the oxtails, place top on and cook on low for
3-4 hours depending on the size of the oxtails. Oxtails will be ready for the veggies when the meat starts falling off the bone. When it has reached that point pour ½ the water off (This takes off more grease) Then add stewed tomatoes, tomato soup, and the rest of the ingredients. All ingredients should be covered with liquid. Cook for about 45 more minutes or until veggies are done.

Niecy's Cornbread Dressing (Stuffing)

NOTE: Make the pan of cornbread the night or two before, cool and refrigerate until ready to make the dressing.

What you will need: Serves 8-10 people
1 lb. chicken gizzards **or** turkey innards (i.e. bag inside the turkey)
Yellow cornmeal for the cornbread (Double the recipe on this)
1 can cream of chicken soup
1 12 oz. bag of sage and onion stuffing squares/cubes
2 eggs (beaten)
Rubbed sage (To taste)
Poultry seasoning (To taste)
Dash of Seasoning salt and black pepper (To taste)
½ cup chopped onion
½ cup celery
2 tbsp. butter (Add more if needed)
One very large bowl or pot for mixing
1 large pot (For chicken gizzards or innards)
Food prep gloves
1 tsp. vegetable oil (To oil the bottom of the roasting pan)
1 medium size roasting pan **or** baking dish to cook the dressing
5-6 cups of broth used from the chicken gizzards or innards.

Before you start, Boil chicken gizzards **or** innards from the turkey with a little salt and pepper, then turn heat down to low and cook 2 ½ - 3 hours with the top on. This will make the broth. Cool and take the meat out and cut some up for your dressing and save some to chop for your gravy. *You're on your own with the gravy! I go by feel and not measuring, using one 1-2 cups of the broth, flour, and browning seasoning.*

In the large pot or bowl crumble the cornbread into to medium size chunks and add the one bag of onion and sage stuffing squares and set aside.

In a skillet melt the butter and add the chopped celery and onion, cook on medium until a soft. Cool the veggies and add them to the cornbread and stuffing squares, then add the can of cream of chicken soup, eggs, and some innards if you decide to use them. Start adding broth in one cup increments starting with 2 cups. After you reach the consistency for baking (a little wet, but not too dry) then add poultry seasoning, rubbed sage, and seasoning salt (Using food prep gloves, mix all ingredients) Making sure not to make mush out of it. Bake at 350 for 30-45 min. until a little brown on top.

No meat option: Use vegetable broth and cream of mushroom soup instead.
(Do not stuff your turkey until you are ready to cook it)

Collard Greens

What you will need: Serves 8-10
1 small smoked turkey leg
6 bunches of collard greens (I like to chop some of the stems on the end into small pieces and put them in too.)
1 dash of seasoning salt
8 cups of water
½ tsp salt
¼ tsp. garlic powder
1 large pot

Instructions: First, take the large middle stem out of the greens and tear greens into about 2x2 inch pieces. Rinse 2 or 3 times depending on how dirty the greens are. Do this by placing the greens in a sink full of water and taking handfuls of greens and dunking them up and down in the water, placing the dunked greens on the other side of the sink with no water in it (If you have a two-sided sink) Drain the dirty water out of the sink, run clean water and repeat. On the 2nd rinse. Open the big end of the salt container and sprinkle back and forth to cover the greens. Let the salt sit on the greens for about 5 minutes, then repeat the dunk rinse. (If there are any bugs they will be at the bottom of the dirty water) Place greens in a pot with the turkey leg and bring to a boil, then turn heat down to low and cook for about 2-3 hours, adding more water if needed. Stir the greens occasionally. They will shrink some as they cook. The turkey will start to fall off the bone, take it out the pot and place it on a plate until it cools. Pull off the skin and take out the bones and place the meat back in the greens. *When the greens are done and ready to serve,* they should **not** be floating in water. (Meaning you should see greens in the pot before you see water). I always cook mine the night before the occasion and put them in the fridge for better flavor the next day. After taking out the fridge taste your seasoning before adding more. Sometimes the smoked turkey leg has more than enough salt in it already.

No meat option: Use liquid smoke and seasonings of your choice
You can also mix Turnip greens and Mustard greens together. My favorite!

That's What's Up Deep Fried Chicken Wings

What you will need:
1 package of chicken wings
1 deep fryer with a basket
1 metal tong
1 bowl with lid
1 gallon plastic baggie for flour
1 cup of flour
Vegetable or Peanut oil (enough to fill halfway in the deep fryer)
Small amounts of:
Seasoning salt
Garlic powder
Garlic salt
Black pepper
1 Timer

For best seasoning results: Wash and dry the wings, and season with seasonings above. Let them sit in a bowl with a top on it in the fridge overnight.

Instructions: Pour access water from the wings off and place wings in the bag with the flour. Shake the bag to coat all parts of each piece of chicken.
In a deep fryer put oil in to fill ½ way on 400 degrees until the oil is hot, about 15 minutes, and leave the top off. *I usually sprinkle a little flour in the oil and when it sizzles like frying chicken, then it is ready for the chicken to go in.*
Add the chicken and turn the fryer down to 350. Cook for about 15-17 minutes **or** until wings start to float in the oil and are golden brown. Place on paper towels to absorb oil.

Alternate: Don't add the flour, and deep fry wings naked with the seasonings above **or** seasonings of your choice. Still crunchy, still good!

Near The Sea Egg Rolls

What you will need: Makes about 15-16 egg rolls
1 large deep fryer with basket
1 medium size pot for mung bean noodles
1-gallon peanut oil or vegetable oil
½ lb. pork shoulder
1 lb. large raw shrimp (devein and cut each into small pieces)
Food processor (Medium size will do)
2 carrots (Grate with small end of the hand grater)
2 small bundles of Mung bean noodles
1 egg (beaten)
1 box of spring roll wrappers (individually wrapped if you can find them)
Salt and pepper to taste
1 medium bowl
1 small bowl
1 large mixing bowl
Cutting board
1 Sharp chef knife
1 small knife
Hand grater
2 large cookie sheets/ One lined with paper towels
Timer
Pastry brush
Food prep gloves

Cut up raw shrimp into small pieces (Devein them), place in medium bowl and set aside. Cut up raw pork shoulder into small squares and place it in the food processor (grind until it looks like ground beef) Take the mung bean noodles and soak in hot faucet water for 15-20 until soft. Place mung bean noodles in a strainer for a couple minutes to drain access water off and paper towel dry. Cut noodles into about ½ inch pieces and place in the large mixing bowl, then add cut raw shrimp, carrots, chopped mung beans, ground raw pork, salt, and pepper. With food prep gloves mix with your hand until all ingredients are well blended. Spoon out one heaping tablespoon per egg roll and spread across making a tube look (See picture) wrap according to the instructions on the spring roll wrapper box and start placing them on the cookie to start the deep fry. Fill up the cookie sheet with all the raw egg rolls before the fry process. In a deep fryer with basket in it, put oil in and fill it ½ way on 400° until it's hot, about 15 minutes then turn it down to 350° once you start to put the egg rolls in.

Deep fry for exactly 7 minutes. You will start to see them turn brown, float, and turn crispy looking. Lift the basket and take the metal tong and remove egg rolls and place them on your other cookie sheet that has the paper towels.

Egg Wash
Beat one egg and one tablespoon of water in a small bowl. Dip the pastry brush in and brush the edges to keep each egg roll from coming apart after you wrap them.

Freezing and Heating
You can freeze any extra eggrolls in foil and place them in a freezer bag.
When you take them out the freezer, they will not be crunchy looking, but they will go back to the original crunchy look by placing them in the oven on a cookie sheet. Place cookie sheet on the middle rack at 400 degrees for 15 minutes. Toaster oven, or air fryer can be used as well. both at 400°.
Heating up in the microwave (not recommended)
Dip egg rolls in egg roll dipping sauce of your choice and enjoy!

Fresh Smoked Turkey

What you will need:
One large black speckled roasting pan with lid **or** roasting pan with foil

Around the holidays you can purchase one from your nearest meat market in advance. This will give the meat market enough time to smoke it if they don't have any ready. Rinse, stuff with dressing, place top on and cook at 325° about 1½ hours or according to the size of the turkey. This one is 10 lbs. You can also put dressing/stuffing inside and bake it.

Delicious!!

Deep-Fryer Naked Crispy Cornish Hen

What you will need:
1 24 oz Cornish hen
1-gallon peanut oil
10 qt. deep fryer with a basket/metal tong
Seasoning of your choice

Place all the oil in the fryer, heat on 400° for 17 minutes. Wash, dry and season the hen. Place the hen the oil and turn heat down to 350°. Fry for 15-17 minutes. When done, the hen will float and also be golden brown. Lift the basket and take the hen out using the metal tong.

Option: *Shake in some flour and deep fry*

Fried Corn

What you will need:
6 ears of fresh corn (shucked)
2 tbsp. Grapeseed oil
Dash of salt and pepper
¼ cup finely chopped bell pepper
¼ cup finely chopped red bell pepper
1 tsp. jalapeño pepper (optional)
¾ cup 2% milk
1 tbsp. sugar
1 large skillet with a lid
1 large deep wide bowl
1 sharp knife and one butter knife (You can also buy a corn peeler and use a butter knife to milk the corn)

In a large deep wide bowl cut corn off the cob with a sharp knife; holding the top of the corn with one hand and cutting downward toward the bowl with the other (Or use a corn peeler). After the corn is off the cob take a butter knife to milk the corn by scrapping up and down the corn a couple times (This is getting the juice out the corn) into the bowl. Heat the oil in the skillet and place the corn in it. Fry on medium high for about 15 min stirring constantly, being careful not to burn it. Add remaining ingredients and pour the milk over the top. Stir and simmer with lid on for about 15-20 minutes, until the milk is cooked off.

Kita's Kickin' BBQ Beans for the BBQ Party!

What you will need: Serves 10-12
3 28 oz. cans of vegetarian baked beans
1.5 lb. package ground turkey
1 small onion (Chopped)
1 small green bell pepper (Chopped)
2 garlic cloves (finely chopped **or** crushed if you're using a garlic crusher tool)
1 dash of garlic salt
1 dash of seasoning salt (Optional)
1 dash of cayenne pepper (Optional)
1 bottle of spicy honey barbeque sauce
1 large skillet
1 large pot

Open the cans of beans and put them in a large pot with a lid and set them aside. In the skillet, crumble the ground turkey, onion, bell pepper, garlic, and seasonings. Cook on medium high until meat is done. Drain fat; put the turkey mixture into the pot with the beans and add barbeque sauce. Stir and turn heat to medium low for about 10 minutes.

Alternate: Mix all into a casserole dish and bake for 15-20 minutes

It's All About Them Crab Cakes!

What you will need:
1 8 oz. container of Blue lump crab meat (Any lump crab will do if you can't find the blue lump crab)
1 egg (Beat)
2 tbsp. mayonnaise
1 tbsp. mustard
1 tsp. seafood seasoning
¼ cup Grapeseed oil
2 ½ tbsp. butter (divided)
½ cup. lightly buttered flavored crackers (Crush them)
¼ cup (**total**) finely chopped celery, red bell pepper, green bell pepper and white onion
1 large mixing bowl
1 large skillet, and one small skillet to sauté veggies
Cutting board
Sauté veggies in the small skillet with a ½ tbsp of butter for about 5 minutes or until veggies are a little soft, then set them aside until cool. When veggies cool mix all the ingredients together, except crabmeat and crushed crackers. Add crab and crackers to mixture last and **mix gently and form into patties.**

Use the other 2 tbsp of butter and put in the skillet with the grapeseed oil. Heat the oil mixture on medium high until hot for about 3 minutes. Place patties in the butter and grapeseed oil mix, and fry 2-3 minutes on each side or until golden brown. See a little brownness around the edges of the crab cakes before turning.

Use mustard on top, or make a Remoulade sauce as shown on the picture.

Baked Potato

What you will need:
1 large russet potato
½ tsp. softened butter
Aluminum foil
1 vegetable scrub brush
1 small baking sheet

Wash potato with veggie scrub brush, Place oven rack in the middle of the oven, preheat oven to 425, place a couple fork holes in the potato on each side with a fork, rub a small amount of softened butter all over it and wrapped in aluminum foil, place on a baking sheet and bake for 50/60 minutes. Slice down the middle and add whatever toppings you like.

Crab cakes

Macaroni and Cheese Please!

What you will need: 6-8 servings
1 16 oz. box of large macaroni
1 12 oz. can evaporated milk
1 egg
salt and pepper (to taste)
Dash of garlic salt and a dash of garlic powder
4 cups shredded triple cheddar cheese blend that includes sharp cheddar in it
1 cup Mozzarella
Pats of butter (Very small chunks)
Paprika
Butter
Non-stick spray cooking oil
2-quart casserole dish
2 medium size bowls
1 whisk
1 strainer

Pre-heat oven to 350°. Boil noodles (Al dente) meaning only 6 minutes. Rinse with cold water and drain macaroni, and set aside. Mix all cheeses together in a bowl and set aside. In another bowl using a whisk mix the milk, egg, salt, pepper, garlic salt, and garlic powder and set aside.
Spray casserole dish with spray cooking oil and layer with macaroni first. Then put about 5 small pats of butter in different places on top of the macaroni.
Take ½ of the cheese mixture and spread evenly on top of the butter and noodles.
Repeat the process (you will be making two layers) on the last layer pour the egg mixture over the top, sprinkle with paprika and bake covered for 30 minutes and uncovered for 10 minutes or until bubbly and golden brown.

Let's Go Down South Fried Oysters

What you will need:
1 16 oz jar of fresh medium/large size oysters
1 ½ tbsp. yellow corn meal
1 cup of all-purpose flour
1 egg (Beaten)
Salt and pepper (To taste)
1 large Cast Iron skillet
Vegetable oil **about an inch** (You want enough to cover the bottom of the skillet and cover only halfway up the up on the oysters)
Metal tong
1 gallon plastic baggie
1 strainer
1 small bowl
Paper towels

Rinse and drain oysters, and add salt and pepper. Place them on a plate and set aside.
Beat one egg with a whisk and put the oysters in the mix and set aside. Place flour, cornmeal, salt and pepper in a baggie and put the oysters in the bag one at a time and shake, covering each oyster before putting the next one in. This is to avoid them from sticking together. Heat oil in the skillet on high for about 5 minutes. Place oysters in the hot oil and turn the heat down to medium high, cooking about 3 minutes on each side. Wait about 3 minutes before turning **or** until you see browning around the edges. If you like them more done cook a couple minutes longer on each side.

Fried Green Tomatoes (Same Recipe as Oysters)
Except; You slice the tomatoes and you won't need a strainer also, no need to shake the baggie as hard.

Still Down South Hot Water Cornbread

You will need:
1 cup of yellow cornmeal
½ cup of flour
Salt and pepper to taste
1 small pot of boiling water
1 heat resistant bowl
Vegetable oil
1 black cast iron skillet
Fork
Metal spatula
Paper towels

In the bowl mix together first, the cornmeal, flour, salt and pepper, then add boiling water until it's the consistency of thick cornbread batter. Place enough oil in the pan to cover the bottom of the skillet about a ½ inch and turn heat on high for about 3-5 minutes to heat the oil. Then turn down the heat to medium and spoon out a ball of batter and mash it down with a fork to form the patty. Cook until it's a little brown around the edges before flipping, then brown the other side (Be careful when flipping, it could splash hot oil) take them out and place on paper towels to absorb access oil.

Let's Go Back Down South Rice Patties

1 cup of cold leftover rice
1 egg
Salt and pepper
1 large skillet
Wide spatula
Non-stick spray cooking oil
1 mixing bowl
1 whisk

Beat together, egg, cold leftover rice, salt and pepper. Spray skillet with a generous amount of spray cooking oil and heat until hot. Turn the heat down to medium and take a couple spoons of mixture and add it to the skillet. Use a fork to lightly mash the mix down just a little to form the patty. There will be more egg on the outside of the patty which is okay, but can also use your spatula and push the egg in some of you like before flipping it over. (Is what I did in the picture) Cook on one side 3 minutes before flipping **or** until it looks like you can flip it (It will be a little light brown around the edges) Cook until lightly brown on both sides. When finished you can choose to put syrup or jelly on them, or eat them plain.

Rice Pattie and Sausage

Mackerel Croquettes

What you will need:
1 15 oz. can of Mackerel
1 egg (beat)
Salt and pepper (to taste)'
1 tsp. seafood seasoning
1/4 cup of flour
1 tbsp. finely chopped yellow onion
1 cup yellow cornmeal
Vegetable oil or Grapeseed oil
1 large skillet
1 large plate
1 medium bowl

Place enough oil to cover the bottom of the skillet about 1 inch. In a medium bowl, combine mackerel, salt and pepper, flour, onion and beaten egg. Pour the cornmeal and spread it out on a plate. Firmly form patties (As many, and big as you like, and set them on the cornmeal. Carefully turn the patties over making sure they are all covered in cornmeal and don break. If you're good, you can pick the patty up and put it in your open four fingers flipping it back and forth in your hands and letting the access cornmeal fall off, if not just sprinkle cornmeal on the other side. Put the oil in the skillet and heat on high for about 3 minutes before adding croquettes. You can tell the oil is hot enough by putting a little cornmeal in skillet and it sizzles like frying. Put the croquettes in and turn heat down to medium. Cook croquettes for 3-4 minutes on each side or until golden brown.
Alternate: Make croquettes for breakfast, with a bowl of grits on the side, adding salt and pepper in them, eggs of your choice, and whole grain toast. *YES!*

Below: Salad: One sliced cucumber, and one sliced tomato. Mixed with a little real mayonnaise, a dash of fresh ground black pepper, and a ¼ teaspoon of vinegar. Place in a serving bowl with a lid, and refrigerate until ready to eat.

Simple Potato Salad
I have never measured this, but it's a very good quesstament.

What you will need:
1 large pot
1 bowl with lid, and one serving bowl with a lid
1 Cutting board
Food prep gloves – Not really, I use my clean hands
4 large russet potatoes
3 boiled eggs (peeled and chopped)
1 dash of seasoning salt (to taste)
Real mayonnaise in one tablespoon increments to the consistency of potato salad you want
Dash of onion powder (to taste)
2 tbsp. sweet pickle relish **or** sweet salad cubes if you can find them
1 tbsp. mustard
Paprika
Strainer

Boil eggs and set aside, until time to add. Peel and cut potatoes into thumbnail size squares, placing them in cold water as you cut them so they don't brown. Strain water, and boil potatoes covered in water on high for about 15 minutes. Pour the hot potatoes in the strainer and run cold water over them right away. Let the water stain and place the potatoes in a bowl with a lid. Put about a tablespoon of mayonnaise in and lightly stir to cover all the potatoes (this is to avoid potatoes from browning) Place the bowl of potatoes with a lid on it in the fridge for about an hour or until cool, before adding the remaining ingredients (This step keeps the potatoes firm and not so mushy) With prep gloves mix the salad by carefully using a circler motion with your hand. Spoon the potato out of one bowl, and spoon into the serving bowl. Sprinkle with paprika.

Spaghetti A La Bukka

You will need: Serves 6-8 (Read instructions fully before starting)
1 16 oz. pk. spaghetti noodles
Water or chicken broth enough to boil noodles
Chicken Boullion if using water for noodles
Olive oil – enough for noodle water and sauté shrimp
1 Chopped red bell pepper
1 Chopped green bell pepper
1 Chopped small onion – white or yellow
4-5 cloves fresh chopped garlic **or** a tablespoon of garlic in the jar – you can never have too much garlic!!
1 8 oz. pk. of mushrooms
Sprinkle a little back and forth once with ingredients below:
Italian seasoning
Garlic Powder
Onion Powder
Seasoning Salt
Pepper
Red pepper flakes (optional)
2 24 oz. jars spaghetti sauce (mix and match, your choice)
2 pkgs – Italian Chicken Sausage **or** 1 pk of beef hot links **or** smoked sausage
1 lb. of raw shrimp (uncooked)
1 8 oz. pk Colby Jack Shredded Cheese – Tillamook is the best but any will do
1 8 oz. pk Medium Cheddar Shredded Cheese
1 8 oz. pk of Parmesan shredded **or** grated parmesan.
Parsley, dry or fresh (optional)
9x13 baking pan

Preheat oven at 350.
In a large pot start boiling broth for spaghetti, add about 2 tbsp of olive oil. Once boiling turn down temp until ready to add noodles, which will be later in the process. Start a small/med pot of plain water to "degrease" sausage. Bring water to boil then simmer. Sausage will be added later.

In a pot or large skillet sauté bell peppers, onion, garlic and mushrooms right before the peppers and onions get soft so they won't overcook. **Season mixture with all the seasonings** until fully cooked. Add spaghetti sauce to veggies, heat to a boil then simmer the sauce.

Slice sausage and add to the small/med pot of hot water you have on simmer, stir a few times until you see the grease rise, then drain and add the sausage to the sauce.

Turn the simmering large pot of water(w/bullion) or broth, and olive oil, up to high until it boils; for spaghetti noodles.

In a medium skillet add enough olive oil to sauté shrimp, sprinkle a little seasoning salt and Italian seasoning and cook. Once cooked do not drain. Add to sauce.
Cook spaghetti noodles according to package directions for 6 minutes.
Simmer sauce.
While noodles are cooking taste and season sauce as needed. May or may not need a bit more seasoning salt and Italian seasoning (Your choice in taste)
Mix noodles and sauce together, well.
Add spaghetti to 9x13 pan
Mix Colby Jack, and Medium Cheddar; sprinkle on top of spaghetti and top it with the parmesan.
Bake 15 minutes; add parsley (optional) and bake another 10-15 minutes until cheese is melted and almost turning brown.

BAM!!!!

My Pan-Fried Prime Ribeye Steak
(*Medium Rare*)

What you will need:
1 1-inch boneless prime ribeye steak
1 12' black cast iron skillet
3 tbsp. vegetable oil
Salt and pepper (To taste)
Garlic powder (To taste)
1 container with a lid to store steak in the fridge
Metal tong
Timer
Cooking thermometer

Prime or aged Ribeye steaks are the most expensive, but they're the best in taste and tenderness.

Wash and dry your steak. Season the steak with salt, pepper, and garlic powder. Place in the fridge in a container with a lid overnight. You will be amazed at how flavorful this is after sitting in the fridge all night!!!

Next day – Let you steak set out in the container to room temperature for 1 hr. before cooking, Heat the iron skillet up for about 3 minutes before adding the oil. Heat vegetable oil up for about 3 minutes on high or until oil is very hot, then add your steak. Turn the heat down to medium high and cook for 3-4 minutes on each side or till the cooking thermometer reaches 130-135 degrees. You should see crisp around the edges before turning it over (use the metal tong to turn the steak.)
Juicy in the middle, and crisp on the outside. So good!
Option: *Grill*

Broiled: Use a butter rub (A very course seasoning of your choice, and soften butter mixed, (1 tbsp each.) Rub it all over the steak or use a marinade. Let the steak sit out of the fridge in the container for 1 hour before cooking. Place the oven rack 2 inches from the top. Pre-heat oven to broil; use a broiling pan with aluminum foil in the bottom portion of the pan. Place the steak on the top of the pan and place it in the oven. Broil for about 3-4 minutes on each side or till it reaches 130-135 degrees on a cooking thermometer for medium rare.

(Above) Pan Fried in a black cast iron skillet
(Below) Broiled with a course steak seasoning butter rub, and grits

From Where I Live Tater Tot Hotdish

What you will need:
1 lb. ground beef or ground turkey
1 medium pot
1 9-inch skillet
1 10.75 oz. can cream of mushroom soup
¼ cup chopped onion
Tater Tots/large or small
1 14 oz. can of French style green beans
Small amount of sharp shredded cheddar cheese (Optional)
8 x 8 baking dish
Salt and pepper (to taste)
¼ tsp. gravy browner in the soup (For the look) if you are okay with the lightness of the soup then you can skip this step.

In the medium pot; cook the soup together with the green beans, and gravy browner, stir gently and set aside. **(Do not add water to the soup)**

Instructions: Brown ground turkey or beef, add salt, pepper. Add onions when the meat is halfway done. When fully cooked, drain and put the meat in the soup mixture and lightly stir. Put all ingredients in the baking dish and spread evenly and place the tater tots on top. Bake according to the instructions on the tater tot package.
When it's done sprinkle a small amount cheese on top and bake until the cheese is melted about 5 more minutes (Optional)

Note: I didn't add salt or cheese to this one. There was enough salt in the can soup.

Tater Tot Hotdish

Wish You Were Here Teriyaki Chicken Drummies/Wings

What you will need:
2 ½ lbs. of drummies **or** one 2-3 lb. package of whole chicken wings
1 large bowl with a lid
1 9x13 pan
Aluminum foil
Metal tong
1 whisk (to mix wet ingredients)
Potato peeler

Sauce

What you will need:
½ cup of low sodium soy sauce
½ cup of oyster sauce
¼ cup of hot oil sauce
1 tsp. finely chopped fresh ginger root (Use a potato peeler to take off the outer skin)
1 tsp. finely chopped fresh garlic

Wash and dry chicken. Mix all sauces and ingredients together in a bowl using a whisk, and place chicken in the bowl with a lid. Refrigerate it overnight till you are ready to cook it the next day. Turn meat at least once to make sure all the meat gets covered at some point. (It will look dark in color for flavor which is okay) Place aluminum foil in the bottom of a pan and bake at 400 degrees (Uncovered) for about an hour depending how big the drummies/wings are. Wings may take a little longer depending on the size. After cooked, cover until ready to eat

NOTE: Double the recipe if using more chicken

Teriyaki Chicken Drummies

What About That Seafood Gumbo!

What you will need: Serves 2-3
1 very large wide mouth pot (I use a black specked one)
1 small pot (For sliced sausage)
Gumbo bowls (Wider mouth bowls)
1 Large long strong spoon (To stir gumbo)
½ bag frozen cut okra
1 can of smoked oysters (drain)
1 16 oz. can stewed tomatoes, including juice (Cut into smaller pieces)
1 16 oz. can tomato sauce
3 beef bouillon cubes
4 cups water
5 crab leg clusters (break legs off cluster body) add the cluster body portion in the pot as well.
2lbs. large **raw** shrimp deveined with tail on (Rinse) *If you really want to make it look good, take the tail off the shrimp, and butterfly them.*
1 bag of some type of crab boil in a bag (do not open the bag)
1 12 oz. ring of turkey or beef smoked sausage **or** beef hotlinks
2 tbsp. of gumbo filè (this thickens and darkens the gumbo.) If you need to add more toward the end to make browner, do so.
1 pot of rice (Cook separately)
Utensils to crack crab, and a picker (A nut cracker set will work)

Slice the sausage and place in some boiling water (stir and pour the water off right away.) It's only to get some of the grease out of the sausage) Set sausage aside until it's time to add the remaining ingredients.
In the large pot add stewed tomatoes, tomato sauce, water, crab boil bag, gumbo filè, and beef bouillon cubes. Bring to a boil then turn down to low and cook for 30 minutes with the top on, carefully stirring occasionally (adding a little more gumbo file if you need to) after 30 minutes pull the crab boil bag out and trash it. Now put crab, shrimp, sausage, okra, smoked oysters, and more gumbo filè if needed. Cook for 25-30 more minutes stirring occasionally. Be sure to stir down to the bottom of the pot, being sure not to let it stick or scorch.
Serve over some rice in a gumbo bowl. (Or be fancy and put some rice on top; using a small bowl, mash the rice down in it. Then place the bowl on top of the gumbo and lift the bowl off. Like shown in the picture. (My rice fell apart a little) Oh well, I tried!

Netta's Veggie Sauté

What you will need:
1 lb. or whole fresh okra (Wash and dry)
10-12 oz. pack of cherry tomatoes (Cut into halves)
1 bunch of Kale (Take out large middle stem) and tear into smaller pieces
1 8 oz. container of white mushrooms (Slice)
Onion powder (To taste)
1 dash Cayenne pepper (Optional)
3 tsp. grapeseed oil
Sea salt
1 tsp. Oregano
1 Large skillet
2 medium size bowls
Cutting board

Wash all veggies and place okra and kale into one bowl, and the remaining prepared ingredients in the other.
Heat oil and place the kale, okra, and seasoning in the skillet first and sauté for 5-7 minutes add the remaining ingredients and cook an additional 5 minutes. So yummy!

Miscellaneous

Punch For the Party!

What you will need:
½ 12 oz. can of frozen orange juice
½ 12 oz. can of frozen lemonade
½ 12 oz. can of frozen fruit punch
2 liters of Ginger Ale
1 pack of any kind of red Kool-Aid
1 orange (sliced)
1 cup of sugar
In a punch bow add all ingredients and fill the rest up with water

NOTE: If spilled on carpet, this will stain.

From Another Island Sofrito Paste

What you will need:
1 Large yellow onion (chop into large pieces)
15 garlic sections (chop in halves)
2 bunches of cilantro (Chopped)
1 bunch of Culantro leaves
2 large green bell peppers (Take out seeds and chop into large chunks)
1 large red bell pepper (Take out seeds and chop into large chunks)
1lb. of Ajices Dulces peppers (Cut in halves and take out seeds) I usually purchase these online
½ tsp. Kosher salt (optional)
1 large food processor
1 large spoon
2 very large pots or bowls
4 oz. mini cups with lids (for freezing)

Separately, in a small pot put:
1 tbsp Annatto Seeds – (Careful this will stain the kitchen counter)
¼ cup Canola oil
Heat until it releases color and add one tablespoon of the yellow-colored oil into the mixture when you're all done. Trash the seeds.

Wash all veggies. Core, and take out the seeds from the peppers. Place all chopped ingredients in a large pot or bowl and put in the food processor in handfuls at a time, and pulse semi coarsely (See picture on the next page). Place all processed veggies in the empty bowl and add the yellow-colored oil mix. Stir together with a large spoon. Using a measuring cup, scoop out portions of the mix and place in small 4 oz. cups with lids and freeze.
Note: 4 oz. size freezing cups are good for a 1-2 serving size of what you are making.

You can find recipes online to season beans, soups, stews, and rice dishes with this.

Turkey Burger with Pepper Jack Cheese

Fruit Salad

Printed in the USA
CPSIA information can be obtained
at www.ICGtesting.com
LVHW060927140224
771416LV00025B/290